POWER OF
THE BLOOD
AT WORK
BROKEN VEIL

Arnetha Thomas

©2011 Arnetha A. Thomas
All rights reserved

ISBN 978-0-9835978-0-3
Library of Congress Cataloging-in-Publication Data

No part of this book may be reproduced, stored
in a retrieval system, or transmitted in any form
or by any means, electronic, mechanical,
photocopying, recording or otherwise without
the written permission of the author.

2NOIT MEDIA AND PUBLISHING
Post Office Box 924212
Homestead, FL 33092
Tel: (786) 200-8149

Editors:Graceiela Sholander
Kionne L. McGhee, Esq.

Book Cover and Design:
eMerge Publishing Group, LLC
Riviera Beach, FL 33404
www.emergepublishers.com

Arnetha A. Thomas, 2011
Power of the Blood at Work "Broken Veil"
1. Autobiographical. 2. Inspirational.
3. Christianity

Printed in the United States of America

CONTENTS

Special Acknowledgments 1

Introduction 5

1 The Growth Process 23

2 The Word Revealed Through Prayer 29

3 Blood Significance and Covenant 35

4 The Old and New Testament
Blood Sacrifice..61

5 Significance of the Broken Veil 73

6 Benefits of the Blood of Jesus 79

7 How to Apply the Power
of the Blood of Jesus 87

Glossary 101

Workbook 103

About the Author 125

Special Acknowledgments

This is my first book and I give special acknowledgment to God for allowing me to get into this place of need, totally depending on Him for my survival. I am most appreciative for the inspiration and insight that He has given me to write this book.

Secondly I must recognize my deceased parents, Leroy and Eunice Thomas. Spiritual growth was always important to my mom, from whom I received the beginnings of my spiritual foundation. She was an adamant churchgoer and, believe me, we attended church every Sunday. I still carry with me a vivid image of the five of us siblings walking to Sunday School in one straight line. Prior to joining the church, our father attended on special occasions, but he would always give us an offering to put into the collection baskets.

Special gratitude and thanks go to Reverend Gerry Latson, former pastor and current Navy Chaplain and certified Marriage and Family Counselor. We are longtime family friends spanning our childhood and adult years at the First Missionary Baptist Church of Brownsville. He was the driving force that probed and provoked my mind to ensure every thought and point were clearly articulated to represent the truth of God's word. The Bible says, "Be diligent to present yourself approved to God, a worker who does not need to be ashamed, rightly dividing the word of truth." (2 Timothy 2:15) Special thanks also go to Dr. Terry Conward, my mentor in spiritual, professional, and personal guidance. I give acknowledgement to Pastor Cecil Lamb for my spiritual development and for helping me believe that I can.

I also give special thanks to Fran L. Thomas, my sister and a certified English teacher, who read this book for grammatical corrections and has supported me in the business with her talents, labor, and money. Special thanks go to my baby sister, Stephanie Thomas, who is supportive and constantly instructs me to stay focused; and to my cousin, Utonda McRae-Frazier, for her support and words of encouragement. Bernadine Bush always challenges me to evaluate and explore every situation and opportunity for maximum positive outcomes. To my publisher, I give special thanks for your diligence and favor in completing this project. To my nieces, nephews, the rest of my family, friends, and to everyone I have inadvertently omitted, I give you thanks because you are important in my life. Many thanks to all of you for reading this book.

It is my prayer that the Power of the Blood at Work and the results of the Broken Veil will equip you with all of God's provisions to overcome your life challenges and situations, including a zeal to live a life that is pleasing to God.

> Scripture taken from the New King James Version
> Copyright 1979, 1980, 1982 by Thomas Nelson, Inc.
> Used by permission. All rights reserved.

Introduction

I wrote this book for several reasons: in obedience to what God told me to do, to be delivered from drowning in my sin, to live in a manner that's more pleasing to God through the power of Jesus' blood and consequently experience His benefits, and to help others understand the character, love, truth, application, and blessings in God's word.

On the morning of Tuesday, September 15, 2009, around 4:45 a.m., while I was praying, the Spirit of the Lord said and reminded me to take the authority that He had given me over those things that were burdening me. The root of it all was a lack of money. This caused me despair. Whenever I thought about my situation and my family's needs. While I prayed, God clearly asked me, "Are you going to sit still and let things just happen?" The Bible says, "Many of the afflictions are of the righteous, but the Lord delivers him out of them all." (Psalm 34:19)

This passage reminds me of what Paul said, "Finally, my brethren, be strong in the Lord and in the power of His might. Put on the whole armor of God so that you and I may be able to stand against the wiles of the devil. We do not wrestle against flesh and blood, but against principalities, against powers, against the rulers of the darkness of this age, against spiritual hosts of wickedness in the heavenly places. Therefore take up the whole armor of God, that you may be able to withstand in the evil day, and having done all, to stand." (Ephesians 6:10-13)

Allow me to give you some background information regarding what compelled Paul to write this letter to the Ephesus church and other believers as a prisoner in Rome. Prior to his imprisonment, he spent over two years ministering to the people in Ephesus (Acts 19:1-10). The people in Ephesus worshipped Diana, the false goddess, and believed that witchcraft, exorcists, and sexual immorality were legitimate parts of their religion. During Paul's ministry in Ephesus and as a leader in the church, he had great influence over the people. Even to the point of causing a riot in that region because people who made and sold idol gods were put out of business (Theological Dictionary of the New Testament).

Therefore, the whole armor of God is the believer's protection during the New Testament time and is still relevant today against evil and the evil one, which is Satan. Paul used the statement "the whole armor of God" as a metaphor in describing the battle dress for a soldier, comparing it to the battle dress for the believer. The battle dress for both consists of a belt, breastplate, shoes, shield, helmet, and sword.

The primary reasons Paul wrote his letter was to equip the Ephesians and other believers with the proper tools to maintain their endurance and their faith in the true and living God, and to protect them from the perverse (sinful) behaviors of their time in those regions, which included the worshipping of false gods, witchcraft, exorcism, and sexual immorality.

Satan has his army of hosts, comprised of people and spirits against God and His righteousness, who operate in the power of darkness by praying to and worshipping that which is evil and not of God. They do so under strongholds including immorality, wickedness, battles of addictive behaviors, lack of self-control, and low self-esteem. This is why Paul said, "We do not wrestle against flesh and blood, but against principalities, against powers, against the rulers of the darkness of this age."

The Ephesians became very strong in Christ, therefore they hated sin and would not allow false teachings and doctrines in the church. Further, they did not tolerate preaching or teaching from leaders who lived contrary to the truth of God's word. Can you imagine all the haters? In this sense, haters are people who do not like you because you do not go along with their wrongdoing, sin, or false teaching.

Therefore, Paul in the New Testament describes the believer's protection and the godly attributes to effectively battle spiritual warfare, to overcome wickedness and negative influences that surround us, and to remain strong in the Lord.

The scripture says, "Stand therefore, having girded your waist with truth." (Ephesians 6:14a) The soldiers girded themselves with a belt around the waist which had strips of leather hanging down to protect their lower body. To gird means to put oneself in readiness for any service that might be required. It was a sign of righteousness and faithfulness (Isaiah 11:5). This symbolizes the importance of the believer to be truthful and honest, and to live a life of integrity. This is the belt of truth.

"Having put on the breastplate of righteousness." (Ephesians 6:14b) The breastplate protected the throat, heart, and vital organs. The breastplate of Roman times went completely around the body, so the back of a warrior was protected. All believers possess the righteousness of Christ. In this instance righteousness relates to practical matters of the heart such as a righteous character and the deeds of believers.

"And having shod your feet with the preparation of the gospel of peace." (Ephesians 6:15a) In battle, the feet were covered by hard studded shoes, where a solid material was set thickly on. It is suggested this represents the preparation of the gospel of peace, or the gospel is the firm foundation that believers stand on; they should be ready to go out and tell everyone about the Gospel (Theological Dictionary of the New Testament).

"Above all, taking the shield of faith with which you will be able to quench all the fiery darts of the wicked one." (Ephesians 6:16) The shield is used against everything. The shield covers or protects the whole armor. The shield offers Christians protection against the fiery darts of the wicked one.

"And take the helmet of salvation, and sword of the Spirit, which is the word of God." (Ephesians 6:17) The helmet protected the soldier's head, and it made him look taller and more impressive. The helmet represents salvation, God's blessings and promises to defeat and overcome whatever situation we may be going through. Then we have the sword representing the word of God to specifically use to cope with and overcome every situation.

The believer's protection consists of truthfulness, honesty, a life of integrity, righteous character and deeds, faithfulness, salvation, and God's specific word to overcome every situation. All of these are still practical for today's Christian. Our protection is not like changing clothes, something that we put on and take off. We must wear the believer's protection daily. We are living in an upside-down society that regards what is right as wrong and what is wrong as right. God hates all sin. The Bible has spelled out sin to include sexual immorality, wickedness, maliciousness, envy, murder, strife, deceit, evil-mindedness, backbiters, haters of God, violent, proud, boasters, untrustworthy, unloving, and unforgiving (Romans 1:29-31).

To stand upright in this evil day of sin, we must daily wear our believer's protection to remain strong in the Lord. Satan wants to overcome, conquer, and control us through our challenges and weaknesses. You see, it is so easy to become involved in sexual immorality by having pre-martial sex or being in agreement with same-sex marriages.

We become evil-minded when we grow jealous of the person who received the promotion, refuse to be a team player, and hope they lose their job. What about the backbiters? These individuals always talk negatively about other people, indulging in gossip. A person who is deceitful lies to have his or her way. The unforgiving heart is responsible for much pain; for example, it was ten years ago when you misunderstood what the other person said, yet you are still angry about the divorce and now take it out on the children. An unloving attitude is characterized by arguing, complaining, or seldom speaking well of your child.

Satan wants us to become bitter and feel that God has turned His back on us. More than likely he wants us to believe that earth is hell and we might as well serve him. You may feel that your sin is not that deep, or that it's just a small sin. Maybe you are guilty of partying most of the time, full of spirits – but not the Holy Spirit. You may value your worldly possessions such as your good looks, car, house, children, and job over God. These types of sins fall into the categories of God-haters, proud, and boasters.

The believer's protection is only for the believer. Without this protection we are prey for Satan to be used for his benefit. You may not know or understand who God is simply due to a lack of knowledge or the fact that nobody has taken the opportunity yet to share the Good News of Jesus with you. Once we get to know who Jesus is and rid the foolish things and ways out of our lives, then we will discover how easy it is to remain strong in the Lord.

Satan thought he had overcome Jesus. In the scripture he took Jesus up on an exceedingly high mountain and showed Him all the kingdoms or nations of the world and their glory and possessions. Satan said to Jesus, "All these things I will give You, if You will fall down and worship me." Then Jesus said to him, "Away with you, Satan! For it is written, 'You shall worship the Lord your God, and Him only you shall serve.'" (Matthew 4:8-10) My thought has always been, What could Satan give Jesus? Absolutely everything–including those kingdoms and possessions–already belongs to God.

Now when we talk about our situations or strongholds, all we have to do is look at Jesus who was hungry and weak because He had not eaten for forty days and forty nights. Jesus defeated Satan by specifically using God's word. If Satan tried to tempt Jesus, he will certainly try to tempt us in our weakness. What about the strongholds of our negative thoughts and imagination, and those situations that we continue to think about that become worse because of our negative thinking? As our parents would say, we're "making a mountain out of a mole hill," which means turning a small something into a big something merely by the way we think. This type of thinking lacks concrete information or evidence. For example, your boyfriend or girlfriend is late calling you, and you begin to say to yourself, "I'm going to tell them a thing or two about their inconsiderate ways." Or you start to believe they may be seeing someone else, when the reality of the situation is that they're stuck in traffic and have no way of reaching you. Again, our thoughts or perceptions are influenced by our negative thinking.

To reiterate, "Therefore take up the whole armor of God, that you may be able to withstand in the evil day, and having done all, to stand." (Ephesians 6:13) God is on our side. He is a God of love. However, He allows us to choose to live for Him or to live for Satan. He lets us choose whether to do what is right or what is wrong. If we choose to live for God, He will help us, give us the power to do what is right, and show us how to overcome our challenges through the believer's protection. Once we make the decision to believe and apply His word, then we can declare the victory through the power of Jesus' blood. He has provided us everything that we need in our battles to defeat our strongholds that may cause us to stumble or fall. As you grow, becoming stronger and faithful through your challenges, remember that the battle has already been won through the power of Jesus' blood. We must now live God's way through our challenges to see the victory come to pass.

Here's another key factor. Jesus gave us the greatest commandment in Matthew 22:37. We need to make it personal: "I shall love the Lord my God with all of my heart, with all my soul, and with all my mind." I love the Lord and desire to love Him more and more. I believe my heart is right. I genuinely love and try to be of help to people. According to my family and friends, I always overextend myself. I am involved in the church, school, and community with many activities, never really taking a break since the next project or the next "thing to do" awaits my attention.

In spite of all my busyness, it feels good to take charge of my destiny as much as I can, even though there is a price to pay. This means a sacrifice of my time, labor, and money, requirements of God. I believe that I am headed in the right direction. Heading in the right direction means you and I must set our goals, determine how we are going to get there, examine our motives, successes, and failures, and make modifications when needed. Then, we continue to move forward, always repeating this process.

"Write the vision and make it plain on tablets, that he or she may run who reads it. For the vision is yet for an appointed time: but at the end it will speak, and it will not lie." (Habakkuk 2:2-3) I find this success principle to be very valuable as it guides me in developing and executing a plan to accomplish any task. Further, this principle is good for coping and managing our daily lives. It is like going to the store with a grocery list to make sure you do not forget anything. Otherwise time may be wasted by returning to the store for forgotten items. So a plan is like a list, a guide to accomplish our goals. I have found myself overwhelmed and seemingly at a standstill in efforts to accomplish my goals, especially without the "Power of the Blood at Work" in my life.

This book is a reminder of what God has already done for you and me through the Power of Jesus' blood. God created us in His image and likeness and to have dominion over the earth (Genesis 1:26). To be made in the image of God includes being sinless like God. He gave Adam, the first man, authority or rule over the earth. When Adam sinned, he gave up his power of authority on earth to Satan. We regained our power through the shed blood of Jesus.

Further, "And we know that all things work together for good to those who are called according to His purpose." This is a blessing for those who love God. The Bible says, "For who He foreknew, He also predestined to be conformed to the image of His Son." (Romans 8:28-29c) What does this mean? God knew us beforehand, and through the power of the shed blood of Jesus, believing Jesus died and rose and our old sinful ways have been forgiven, we are made new and righteous like Christ. Christ knew no sin, but gave His life for us as a sin offering to bring us back to the right relationship with God. We also regained our authority and dominion over the earth.

Earlier we said God created us in His image. Do you believe this? Do you believe our purpose on earth is to serve and please God? Will we be like many of the Israelites, not obtaining our purpose or promise because of disbelief and disobedience?

"Then the Lord said, 'I have pardoned the people's sins according to your words Moses, but truly, as I live, all the earth shall be filled with the glory (or magnificence) of the Lord, because all these men who have seen My glory and the signs which I did in Egypt and in the wilderness, and have put Me to the test now these ten times, and have not heeded My voice, they certainly shall not see the land of which I swore to their fathers, nor shall any of those who rejected Me see it.'" (Numbers 14:20-23)

After all God had done for the children of Israel, including delivering them from slavery in Egypt, parting the Red Sea, keeping them from sickness and disease, feeding them in the wilderness, and defeating their enemies. In spite of all the signs and wonders given by God that the people witnessed, the Israelites continued to sin and disobey God by not believing in Him and worshipping false gods. The consequence of their wrongdoing was that many of them did not enter the Promised Land.

In my lifetime I have heard stories of people healed from sickness. God allowed me to lay hands on my sore throat and at that very moment I was healed. I kept swallowing to confirm it was true, and so it was. Since that time more than two years ago,

I experienced a sore throat only briefly on two occasions.

Around the latter part of last year, I was sulking in my car with my head down at the red light, complaining about my no-money situation to God. He allowed me to look up in time to avoid hitting someone's car from behind, saying to me, "I got your back." This was an awesome experience for me that increased my faith in God. I read my Bible, remembering His power and might. However, as time continued my faith and belief system weakened, lacking power, and I continued to find myself in need of money.

To only believe is insufficient. I must put my belief into action, which to me is a lifestyle of becoming more connected to God. I have cheated myself by not building a more connected relationship with God to allow the results of the Power of the Blood in my life to work more effectively. Most importantly I cheated myself by being so tired and not putting God first: Lying in bed knowing I'd be falling asleep before finishing my prayer. Brainwashing myself to believe I could pray a prayer of breakthrough while in bed. This has not worked for me, especially since I am not physically handicapped and I know what God requires of me. What does He require of you?

Here's another point: How can I say that the Lord is my strength in whom I will trust (2 Samuel 22:3) and God shall supply all my needs according to His riches in glory by Christ Jesus (Philippians 4:19)? I have found myself "hitting and missing," in other words, not feeling, believing, or understanding the impact of God's words and power including the authority He has given by praying. Therefore, I have become weak because of an inconsistent prayer life lacking in earnestness and steadfastness. The opposite of this is a consistent prayer life, leading to increased manifestations of God's blessings.

Then I will operate in His strength, power, and authority, knowing without a doubt that He supplies all of my needs. It is important to carve out personal time with God, regardless of our situations, agendas, or what we may be going through. Then we can truly say the Lord is our strength and supply. I continuously thank God for His love, grace, and mercy. In spite of my shortcomings He is still on my side. God sees something good in each one of us because of His love and the power of Jesus' blood.

One may ask, who is God? There are so many names and descriptions of who God is. Asaph was a priest and choir member who said that "the Mighty One, God the Lord, has spoken and called the earth from the rising of the sun to its going down." (Psalm 50:1) This represents God's majestic power. Remember that God chose Moses to lead the Israelites out of Egypt and spoke to Moses by saying, "I am the Lord. I appeared to Abraham, to Isaac, and to Jacob, as God Almighty, but by My name Lord I was not known to them." (Exodus 6:2-3) So, who is God to you, or who do you know God as? It is a personal thing. I know God as my Comforter and Helper in times of trouble.

There is a possibility that you don't know Him or you desire to know Him more. If you don't know Him, say the following, "I believe Jesus died on the cross for my sins and rose from the dead." (Mark 16:6) Then say, "God, I want to know you. Please help me, and come into my heart." If you desire to know Him more, ask God to increase His presence in your heart and say, "God, I love you." The scripture says, "God desires all men to be saved and come to the knowledge of truth." (1Timothy 2:4) God wants a special relationship with all of us and desires we grow in knowing Him. He is a God of love and His love for us is unconditional.

In this book I will share my life experiences through the application of God's word. I pray that from reading the Power of the Blood at Work and the results of that power through the "Broken Veil" you will gain a fuller understanding of what God is doing and desiring to do for you in your life, family, and friendships.

The Growth Process

Life leads us into situations where we can go through the motions, be dead while still living, or really live. I will explain what I mean through the following example. On one of my jobs, I realized that my position could be eliminated because very capable, qualified people working under me were doing most of the work. I could have said, "Oh well, what can I do?" and just gone through the motions. Even more, I could have been dead while still living by becoming unproductive, bitter, angry, and jealous of my co-workers. What I decided to do, however, was to really live by becoming more marketable. I enhanced my skills through training and developed expertise to the point where I became more beneficial to my employer. God directed my pathway in this situation.

What do we do when situations seem to be so unbearable? Say, for instance, that we started a business and find ourselves at the point where, after almost two years, there is still not enough money coming in from the business. We have the qualifications, credentials, and expertise, and we are believers in Christ Jesus. What do we do? We still trust God. Paul says, "No temptation has overtaken you except such as is common to man; but God is faithful, who will not allow you to be tempted beyond what you are able, but with the temptation will also make the way of escape, that you may be able to bear it." (1Corinthians 10:13)

My interpretation of this scripture is that everybody goes through something, but God is faithful, and He always makes a way of escape. He provides options or allows us to have patience while going through a difficult situation. I believe God gave me an escape a long time ago from my frustrations, challenges, and business failures. I did not hear Him because He did not have my full attention. I believe He was with me, but I was not with Him. I was too busy to hear Him and failed to carve out consistent time with Him in prayer.

In the midst of my spiritual decline, stuff just continued to happen with my finances in both the personal and business sides of my life. I said, "Well God, it is all about helping your people." However, in believing this, I continued blessing others with my service and money when I had it to give. God did not let me fail or just completely fall apart even though my frustrations continued. I would tell myself, making it personal, "I walk by faith, not by sight." (2 Corinthians 5:7) "But do you want to know, O foolish man, that faith without works is dead?" (James 2:20) I was foolish in the sense of not giving God more attention and not acting on what He had given me to do.

Now as I think about it, I believe the assignment that He gave me is a way of escape that will meet the needs of His kingdom, my personal life, and our business. What is meeting the needs of God's kingdom? It is telling others the "Good News" that Jesus lives and that He loves us. It is helping to spread the Gospel and to assist through giving. Nevertheless, I continued operating my life according to my will and way. I wrote grants, built social networks, and contracted my services.

How many of you know there was no change in my situation or finances? Yes, you are right! Savings continued to deplete, and we all know that savings are finite, not a bottomless pit. We understand the principle of everything going out and nothing coming in; the supply will eventually dry up. I would think about this often and would say to myself many times that God is concerned about people. Therefore I continued doing things my way and continued to experience lack. Our business partners failed to pay us on time and currently owe us money.

Oh my God! The telephone would ring off the hook from creditors. At some point I stopped answering the phone. I got tired of repeating the same old story of why I was unable to pay my bills. Believe it or not, most of my creditors were nice. They had some sympathy for me, but they wanted their money. I must acknowledge that two staff continued to work for free. The younger ones moved on but helped out when needed. They have young families with responsibilities, and those of us who stayed on are older people with responsibilities.

Since I had a few dollars to sustain us for a season, I continued not to really hear God. I did not act on the assignment He gave me. In the next chapter I will share the assignment with you. However I must truly say how thankful I am for the savings He made available to me. As mentioned earlier, God knew a time like this was coming. He knows my temperament and my heart. In spite of my ways He has continued to bless me, even though I have not as of yet obtained all He has for me because of disbelief and disobedience. You remember the story of the Israelites, the ones that did not obtain all God had for them because of their disbelief and disobedience.

Finally I began to reach the bottom of the pit, forcing me to get on my face and come to the realization that God's riches and resources are bottomless and everlasting. Then I was ready to hear and apply God's Word to my life. He brought me to the remembrance that I failed to truly love Him with all of my heart, mind, and soul. If I had been doing this all along, I believe His power would have truly reigned earlier in my life, especially for the financing of our business.

Therefore, my growth process started in my disobedience that caused me to believe in myself and my resources. This experience was necessary for my spiritual development. Secondly, I realized my resources are limited while God's resources are unlimited. Third, I repented and poured out my heart, which means I talked to God about everything including the business, finances, and family. My prayers are sincere and my growth process continues daily as I routinely praise, worship, thank God, repent, make my request known, and declare the victory. My prayers are also informal. I talk to God while in the car, in my bed, at work, everywhere and anytime I need His help, have a question, need to repent, think about Him, or just want to thank Him.

The Word 2
Revealed Through Prayer

I knew God was speaking to me through prayer. On many occasions after I prayed, He gave me spiritual topics that I wrote down and studied. At some point during my study I said, "This is too time-consuming. My God, I see what a preacher has to go through." I felt so busy that studying and writing about these topics took too much of my time. Therefore I pushed His work to the side. God's word lay on my bed for a long time and then became buried among papers in my bedroom.

I wrote salvation tracks that I was supposed to hand out to men and women whenever they came to my car to ask for money. The salvation tracks were poems in everyday language to get people to think about their lives and God. I did not complete this project. I did put together bags of toiletries and other personal items for those who approached my car in need. At some point I was not focused, I stopped writing the tracks, and I stopped handing out the bags. Since I was disobedient and primarily for not putting God's work first, He discontinued giving me His word through prayer to write about. I was possibly so consumed in what I was doing that I stopped listening.

I recently found my tablets and some of the topics that He gave me were dated 2006, 2007, and the last was 2008. At least four years ago, the subjects centered on famine, pilgrimage, favor, and the Gospel. I am also reminded that I was given a prophecy about ten years ago that I would be a pastor of a church. Well, the truth is, I am learning not to discard God's work or take His word lightly, but instead allow Him to lead me in the path that I should go. The more I think about it, it is not what I think. So let me rephrase this thought: God's work is beyond the confinement of a building, and I will seek Him for clear direction.

Time continued to pass by, and as you already know we run a business that is also very time-consuming. Our focus is conflict resolution and reconciliation and again, God has blessed me in this area with expertise. I started writing books for the business. However, I couldn't get it together to write or finish these books or related helping tools for the public. Then a "light" came on and revealed to me that I will not be able to complete any books or tools for the business until I put God's work first.

Almost immediately through prayer God gave me a revelation about the Power of the Blood and I wrote down what He said, which was to apply this over my situation. I prayed the Power of the Blood over my finances, business, family, church and personal life in Jesus' name. I ended the prayer "in Jesus' name" because He said, "If you ask anything in My name, I will do it." (John 14:14) I became so excited because I could hear God speak to me again. He told me to feel better and to renew my strength in Him by praying and believing His word that I would be blessed in those areas I need help in. When God speaks to me I can hear His voice so clearly. Other times His thoughts just come into my mind.

God gave me another chance to obey Him. I realized God wants all to be saved and none lost. His word says, "But seek first the kingdom of God and His righteousness, and all these things shall be added to you." (Matthew 6:33) One example of seeking

God's kingdom first is attending the church's prayer shut-in instead of going to a family gathering or going on a date. The prayer shut-in is the opportunity to hear from God and receive direction for our lives, build a loving relationship with God, and strengthen relationships among the members of the body of Christ. I believe once we seek God's kingdom first, we are closer to receiving the desires of our hearts such as a better job, a husband, a wife, salvation for others, and financial blessings.

Power of the Blood at Work was not difficult to write since I truly believe this book is an inspiration to me from God. In addition, all of my life experiences, relationships, Sunday School teachings, family, and friends have impacted and influenced my life and the contents of this book.

I had written most of the book but stopped because I needed a closing. Then I traveled to Washington, D.C. with my high school classmates. The purpose of our trip was to be in the celebration atmosphere of President Obama's first year in office. The trip was a blessing in many ways. I was grateful when my airfare and hotel were generously paid for by my classmate. I was humbled when I received the closing for this book. I had gotten up early that morning to pray, and it was during this time that God gave me the closing. Once I received this information, I thought the book was finished. However, I was challenged to present myself approved by God as a workman rightly dividing the word of truth. Therefore, it took me approximately two more weeks to finish God's book.

So now I am "on fire," having a craving like never before. Think about your favorite food or passion, the way you feel about your children, or how that man or woman that you love makes you feel. This is how I feel in having the desire to finish this book and to see God at work in my life. How compassionate, wonderful, and magnificent God is. "It is good to give thanks to the Lord, and to sing praises to Your name, O Most High; to declare Your loving kindness in the morning, and Your faithfulness every night." (Psalm 92:1-2) This is praising God, recognizing who He is and how great He is.

God's desire is to speak to all of us through prayer. If you are not hearing from God, this could be for reasons such as disobedience, inconsistent prayer, too busy, or a lack of faith in God. Paul says, "Pray without ceasing." (1 Thessalonians 5:17a)

This means to maintain a faithful prayer life by being persistent and consistent in prayer.

If we want to hear God and know it is Him we are hearing, Daniel provides us with a perfect example. He prayed to God three times a day (Daniel 6:10). Read about the visions, dreams, and the favor God gave Daniel. God desires to do the same for you and me. What are your visions or dreams? How much do you want to hear from God? Do we want more power, a closer relationship, the favor and blessings of God? I do, which is why my prayer life has increased by praying in the morning, becoming more consistent about it before I go to bed, and praying when I wake up during the night to intercede for others. However, it is still a growth process. What about your prayer life?

Blood 3
Significance and Covenant

According to Leviticus 17:11, "For the life of the flesh is in the blood, and I have given it to you upon the altar to make atonement for your souls; for it is the blood that makes atonement for the soul." This verse is saying that the life of animals and humans are in the blood. If a creature loses its blood, it loses its life. God appointed the blood as an atonement or offering for the sins of humans that originated from the sin of one man, Adam. This original sin resulted in a broken relationship between Adam and God (Genesis 3:23-24), affecting all people.

Before God instituted the sin offering, there are incidents in the Bible where God killed people because of their sin, wickedness, and outright disobedience to Him. This sounds so cruel, and I'm very happy that I was not living during that time. Examples include the flood (Genesis 6:11, 17), Sodom and Gomorrah (Genesis 18:20, 19:13), the death of Er (Genesis 38:7), and the death of Onan (Genesis 38:8-10).

Until the one-time sacrificial blood offering of Jesus, God temporarily required a sin offering from the people by the blood of animal sacrifices. A life was given for a life as an offering for the sins of people who had to be renewed constantly. However, animal sacrifices could never take away sins (Hebrews 10:4).

The correlation and significance of the blood in our body and for our soul are so awesome that it can only be orchestrated by God, the Almighty. The blood is a sustainer of life in both realms of the body and soul. Subsequently, the significance of the blood is two-fold.

In our body the blood contains many vital nutrients that are essential to the proper functioning of our organs such as the heart, kidneys, and brain. The blood is responsible for our oxygen, keeps our body warm and cool as needed, fights off infections,

POWER OF THE BLOOD AT WORK "BROKEN VEIL" 37

and rids waste. Without blood and its nutrients, there is no human life.

Our soul is where we sin, causing us to be disconnected from God. Our soul is our intellect, will, and emotions. It is in this area that we operate according to the lust of our eyes, indulging in those things that make us feel good. The battle is against sin and evil. In the Bible, God called the people of Israel stiff-necked, meaning they were stubborn, disobedient, and wanted their own way (Exodus 33:4-5). When Moses was out of their sight, the people made and worshipped false gods, having a big party (Exodus 32:1-6).

What about today's Christian? How do we behave in our daily living? What about when things do not go our way? Some people are constantly complaining, failing to be a team player at work, home, or in the church. Some too easily are ready to, or already have succumbed to, cursing at another person. It does not seem to matter what ground they are standing on. For example, it could be holy ground, the church.

But do you know that wherever our feet tread or walk upon, we should always demonstrate behavior that is pleasing, holy, and acceptable to God (Romans 12:1)? I am not saying that we do not have emotions or feelings, but as believers our walk and talk should be different. We are expected to demonstrate the character of a new person in Christ with attributes such as kindness, humility, bearing (tolerance) with one another, and forgiving. Dr. Martin Luther King, Jr., one of the greatest nonviolent leaders and kingdom builders, talked about agape love that is unconditional.

As believers in Christ Jesus we are His chosen people and heirs to God's covenant. The covenant includes blessings for your children and your children's children because of your righteousness (Deuteronomy 4:40; 5:29). Do you want the blessings for your children and your children's children? Knowing that all is well with my son, grandchild, and the generations to come, fills my heart with joy and peace.

Many of today's Christians are not fully committed to God. They may believe that, since they put God first by attending church on Sunday or on their day of worship, they have fulfilled their duty. Afterwards they figure it is their time to relax and drink their alcoholic beverages. Many believers drink any day of the week and feel that drinking is a normal part of life when it comes to entertaining family and friends. Some drink socially, while others do so for stress relief. Some may casually drink one glass of wine, while others may drink several glasses or an entire bottle of liquor. Some drink to rid themselves of stress or problems, only to discover no change in their situations. Drinking is one negative behavior many embrace in a futile attempt to cope with challenges. Other negative behaviors people turn to as a coping mechanism include fornication, adultery, and lying, but all of these are only temporary fixes at best. These are not much different from the temporary animal blood sin offerings that had to be done repeatedly and were of no value in the long run.

God has provided a new and better way, a one-time sacrifice which is Jesus. This is your time to realize the importance of the blood and accept God's way of righteousness. He has a better way for you to live and cope with life situations. Ask Him to help you and He will show you His way. My purpose is not to condemn, but to challenge all of us to examine ourselves and live to please God.

In Leviticus it was already said that the Israelites were stiff-necked people who worshipped false gods. Therefore they had to present an animal sacrifice to the priest for the atonement of their sins repeatedly. The atonement was a process and responsibility of the priest. If the priest had sinned, he had to offer an animal blood sacrifice for himself first. According to my study Bible, when the Israelites brought their animal sacrifices to the door of the tabernacle, they were identified as worshippers (Leviticus: 4:4-5).

In modern-day times, when we sin and go before God in prayer for repentance, each of us should present ourselves as a worshipper who is humble, reverent, and serving God. Worship is defined as, "The adoring acknowledgement of all that lies beyond us, and the glory that fills heaven and earth. It is the response that conscious beings (believers) make to their Creator, to the Eternal Reality from which they came forth." (Evelyn Underhill).

"But the hour is coming, and now is, when the true worshipers will worship the Father in spirit and truth; for the Father is seeking such to worship Him. God is Spirit, and those who worship Him must worship in spirit and truth." (John 4:23-24) In other words, to worship God in spirit is having divine communion with Him. Worshipping is a matter of the heart and truth coming into harmony with the nature and will of God. We connect to God in the spirit by meditating on how good, loving and kind He is, and when we declare Him to be the Alpha and

Omega, the beginning and the end of our life. Thanksgiving to God should be in our hearts.

Going back to the topic of sin, Jesus the Christ is the one-time and better sacrifice for the atonement or offering for our sins. His blood is the sustainer of our soul, and in the Old Testament His coming is predicted. This prophecy is confirmed in the New Testament. The Old Testament says, "But He (Jesus) was wounded for our transgressions (sin or violation in ignorance), He was bruised (beaten) for our iniquities (sin or wickedness);" see Isaiah 53:5. In the New Testament, "Whom God set forth as a propitiation (offering) by His blood, through faith, to demonstrate His righteousness, because in His forbearance (supernatural being) God had passed over the sins that were previously committed (sins of the people before Christ's death);" see Romans 3:25. "But now in Christ Jesus you who once were far off have been brought near by the blood of Christ." (Ephesians 2:13) Many other Bible scriptures and more evidence support the significance of blood for the atonement of mankind's sins. Without the blood, there would be no new covenant.

Earlier we mentioned covenant, which is an agreement or a promise. We will discuss the covenants made by God to the people and will begin with Abram, which means "exalted father." God told His servant, "Get out of your country, from your family and from your father's house, to a land that I will show you. I will make you a great nation; I will bless you and make your name great; and you shall be a blessing … in you all the families of the earth shall be blessed. So Abram departed as the Lord had spoken to him, and Lot went with him. Abram was seventy-five years old when he departed from Haran." (Genesis 12:1-3a, 4) God gave Abram a commandment; as a result of his obedience God made a covenant (promise) with him.

How many of you know God wanted to do something great with Abram? When He told him to move, Abram was obedient. This is how it should be with us when we receive an order from God. Directives come from God through the pastor, prayer, prophecy, reading the Bible, dreams, and visions. If you are unsure about a directive such as helping others, supporting a ministry, which job to take, a plan of action, or a question concerning your children, go to God in prayer for guidance and confirmation. Most times the answer is very clear in the Bible, giving direction to God's people. Many times we already know or have been given the directive, but we need guidance, confirmation, or reassurance. Then we can ask God for a sign.

Read the Bible story about Gideon starting at Judges 6:11 and going through Judges 8:21, where the Angel of the Lord appeared to him and said, "The Lord is with you, you mighty man of valor!" The Lord told Gideon, "You shall save Israel from the hand of the Midianites." The conversation went back and forth, like a parent talking to a child who is in disbelief. Finally Gideon said to the Lord, "If now I have found favor in Your sight, then show me a sign that it is You who talk with me." The Lord gave a sign and Gideon said, "Alas, O Lord God! For I have seen the Angel of the Lord face to face." This was not the only sign God gave Gideon, because he asked for more signs. He asked God not to be angry with him, and his requests were granted. God wants to do the same thing for us. He wants us to talk with Him concerning directions and confirmations for our lives. We must be sincere when we approach God. It took Gideon a while, but he listened. Are we listening to God?

Back to Abram, God had already promised Abram that He will make him a great nation and that he will have a son. Abram and his wife, Sarai, were well past child-bearing age. Subsequently, as time went forth and considering their old age, they seemed to have become weary, tired of waiting. Therefore Abram listened to Sarai and fathered his wife's maid's son, Ishmael. Later God changed Abram's name to Abraham, the father of many, and said, "As for Sarai your wife, you shall not call her name Sarai, but Sarah shall be her name." Just as God had previously told Abram, He again explained, "I will bless her and also give you a son by her; then I will bless her, and she shall be a mother of all nations." (Genesis 17:15-16b) I am sure Abraham and Sarah realized they moved in haste instead of seeking God more or asking Him for a sign.

This is how we are sometimes, trying to fix things ourselves only to make matters worse. It is suggested that we seek God first before making decisions that will seriously impact our lives, or simply read the Bible for instructions on how to live. In many instances we are already aware that some of the choices we make in life are neither pleasing to God nor good for us. For example, we choose the wrong mate to marry. They were not right from the beginning, but we felt that we could change them. That was a poor choice on our part. However, once in the relationship, it's important to ask God for direction and to model righteousness.

Another example: Let's say we decided to have our babies outside of marriage. Then we fall out with our boyfriend or girlfriend and do not get along with each other, hurting the children. In spite of our terrible decisions and messed-up situations, God still loves us and continues to bless us. Blessings can come in different forms. Perhaps the relationship was restored and the parents married. The children may have been raised without marriage and developed into good children that were obedient at home, did well in school, and/or accomplished their goals. For that child who has been disobedient, we must continue to pray and never give up. Read the story about the prodigal son in Luke 15:11-24. The main point of this story to me is that "he came to himself."

Returning to Abraham, just like God said, Isaac the promised heir or son was born to Sarah and Abraham in their old age. Abraham was obedient when God asked for his son Isaac as an offering. He did not withhold his son and God provided Abraham with a sacrifice in place of Isaac. Then God said to Abraham, "Blessing I will bless you, and multiplying I will multiply your descendants as the stars of the heaven and as the sand which is on the seashore; and your descendants shall possess the gate of their enemies. In your seed all the nations of the earth shall be blessed, because you have obeyed My voice." (Genesis 22:17-18)

Abraham's descendants are the Israelites, the group of people who outnumbered the Egyptians and were led out of bondage in Egypt by Moses. We are in the process of seeing the covenant made by God to Abraham fulfilled. Genesis 37 begins the history of the Israelites arrival in Egypt and continue reading about their lives and deliverance from bondage.

We are now on the scene with Moses, telling the people how God will bless them if they obey His commandments. He said, "So you shall serve the Lord your God, and He will bless your bread and your water. And I will take sickness away from the midst of you… And I will send hornets before you, which shall drive out the Hivite, the Canaanite, and the Hittite from before you." (Exodus 23:25, 28) Remember, they were in the wilderness, something like a jungle, and God basically said, "I will take care of you, give you water to drink, and you will never go hungry." Hornets are insects with a terrible sting that God said He would use to drive the people out the land promised to the Israelites. Think about the wilderness, jungle, or junk in our lives. God said

He will take care of us in the midst of our junk and situations, if we just serve Him. So, with obedience there is a promise.

Some of us may be asking: How can God put the people out of their land? This may seem so cruel, but remember, the earth and everything in it, including the land, belongs to God. Further, He promised the land to the descendents of Abraham because of his faithfulness and obedience. Let us think for a minute; many of our blessings are not because of our righteousness, but results from the faithfulness and obedience of our ancestors, such as our mothers, fathers, grandparents, great-grandparents and so forth.

The scripture continues by saying, "I will not drive them out from before you in one year, lest the land become desolate (or uninhabited) and the beasts of the field become too numerous for you. Little by little I will drive them out from before you, until you have increased, and you inherit the land." (Exodus 23:29-30) Moses told the people all the words of God and His judgments. The people agreed to do all that He commanded.

God said, "Little by little I will drive them out from before you, until you have increased, and you inherit the land." My understanding of this verse is that God knows what we need for success. He was looking out for the children of Israel. The latter should be compared to a parent's responsibilities of caring and raising children for adulthood. One more illustration of preparation is when we obtain a new job. The supervisor or manager is responsible for the new employee's orientation and training towards independency.

The Israelites were not yet at the capacity to manage. They were neither equipped, nor large enough in number to handle all God had for them. In today's society, the latter would equate to God trusting someone with a million dollars when they have not demonstrated their ability to handle fifty thousand dollars. Further, we are speaking about the importance of reaching a point of maturity in handling increase or moving to the next level. How many of you know one has to be ready? We must be prepared, in position, equipped, and with the right attitude when we begin to receive more of God's blessings.

In our lives, and I look at mine in particular, I've wondered why it has taken so long to acquire finances to support the business, have a husband, and obtain breakthroughs for family members in job opportunities and relationships. You may be asking

God for a wife, house, car, or healing in your body. I realize our lives are predestined by God and He is all-knowing. Even though our lives are predestined by God, our receiving what He has for us is based upon our obedience. Without total obedience, we can receive some of our blessings, but not all of them. Nevertheless, I've sometimes wondered and asked God, what's going on? How much longer? When, Lord?

I am more convinced that "little by little" includes the preparation phase before we see a fuller manifestation of God's blessings. My preparation phase includes trusting God more to meet my needs, increasing my prayer life, being obedient, and having patience. God already knows the end before the beginning, but He wants you and me to confidently know without a doubt that we are in position to handle and receive His blessings. The blessing of the Lord makes one rich, and He adds no sorrow with it (Proverbs 10:22).

Regardless of our disappointments and setbacks, we must believe God's word for our finances and relationships. Whatever we believe God for, and to have true success according to God's standards, our beliefs must be in line with His will. His blessing makes us rich in every area of our lives. This means our spirit, soul, and body. Our spirit is our divine nature that belongs to and communicates with God. Our soul is our mind, intellect, and emotions. Our body is our physical wellbeing. God wants us to worship Him in spirit and in truth (John 4:24). Additionally, He wants us to prosper in good health as our soul prospers (3 John 2).

God still wants to bless us regardless of our personal or spiritual state in life. He is waiting on us and it is not too late if you are reading this book. One must repent, begin to trust God for all our needs and desire, moreover to read His word. Most importantly, we must pray the power of the blood of Jesus daily over our lives and circumstances.

What about God's servant, Job? Satan appeared before God and was asked what he thought about Job. After all, Job feared God, was blameless, lived an upright life, and was the richest in the East. Satan told God that if He removed His protection from around Job, the man would curse Him to His face. Subsequently, God allowed Satan to attack Job's character, health, and possessions, but not take his life. Within this ordeal Job talked about his righteousness and all that he did, and he cursed the day that he was born. He did not curse God. Job was rebuked, or put down, by his three old friends. His wife told him to curse God and die. Finally, Elihu of the Ram family, an ancestor of King David (Job 32:2; Ruth 4:19), stood nearby, heard what was said, and in common day language indicated: "Enough is enough."

In anger, Elihu told Job that he was justifying himself instead of God. Job said, "I am pure, without transgression, I am innocent, and there is no iniquity or sin in me. Yet He (God) finds occasions to be against me." Do we sometimes think like Job when we are going through difficult times? We fail to closely examine ourselves, take some responsibility for our actions, or wait on God to see the intended outcome.

Even though God said there is none upright like Job, he still was not perfect. Elihu was in agreement and told Job, "You are not righteous." Job was exalting himself and I am sure that at some point, he burnt a sin offering for himself. Elihu said, "God is greater than man." His message to Job was: if you are so righteous, what do you give God and what does He receive from your hands? Why do you contend or compete with Him? For God may speak in one way, or in another. Yet man does not perceive or understand it. God may speak in a dream, a vision of the night when deep sleep falls upon men and women slumbering in their beds. Then He opens the ears of those that He chooses and seals their instructions. Elihu reminded Job that God is great and we do not know Him. Nor can we number His years of existence (Theological Dictionary of the New Testament).

Elihu was angry with Job's three friends because they found no answer for Job's situation. They continued to condemn him. God's anger was also aroused against Job's friends since they did not speak what was right about God or His servant Job. God commanded these friends to take seven bulls and seven rams and go to Job to offer up for themselves a burnt offering for their sin and Job would pray for them. Let this be a lesson for all of us. Whenever we are going through trials and tribulations, we must never exalt ourselves or brag that we are so righteous or without sin. In addition, we are not to point fingers and accuse others because of their situation. We should listen more, accuse less, and speak well of others if we can, or else say nothing. I must continue to work to improve in these areas. The Bible says we should love our neighbor as we love ourselves (Leviticus 19:18b) and this includes everyone.

In Job we see that Satan still has access to God (Job 1:6-7) and goes before Him daily speaking negatively about us. Satan seeks to challenge God in removing His hand of protection from around us. Satan's belief is simple: if His hand is removed, we will curse God. For the record, the devil is a lie and the truth is not in him. We are God's people, who are living or striving to live righteously. Nevertheless we should be like Job who continued to love God and accepted his friends' apologies for false accusations. We should pray for those who spitefully use us and talk about us. Finally, we should not be filled with so much pride that we cannot ask for forgiveness when we wrong others and/or accept others' apologies. As a result of Job's obedience in the form of accepting his three friends' burnt offerings, praying for them, and repenting to God for his wrongdoing, he was forgiven. Job's losses were restored and he gained much more. Read the story of Job to achieve a fuller understanding of his anguish and restoration.

I mentioned the preparation phase earlier. Hopefully we can recognize this phase when we are in it, since life is a learning cycle of new experiences and challenges. Nevertheless, Paul tells us what type of attitude or character we should display. "Not that

I speak in regard to need, for I have learned in whatever state I am, to be content. I know how to be abased (suffer need) and I know how to abound (or have plenty). Everywhere and in all things I have learned both to be full and to be hungry, both to abound and to suffer need. I can do all things through Christ who strengthens me." (Philippians 4:11-13)

When we read about Paul's life, the Bible states that he persecuted the church and believers in Christ. During that time, his name was Saul and he thought his behavior was approved by God. However, when he heard the voice of the Lord, he was obedient and submissive, and he became an advocate of Jesus the Christ. God gave Saul an identity change in name and character. His name became Paul and he was a kingdom builder for God. This change came from the power of the blood as a confessed believer in Christ Jesus.

In my preparation phase I needed a character change even though my name is still Arnetha. Do you need a character change? What do we do when we hear the voice of the Lord? Were you like me and did not hear Him anymore? Do we listen, become obedient, and submit to what God is saying? Are we obedient like Paul? We may not be physically knocked off a horse like Paul was, or blinded by a shining light (Acts 9:3-15), but we may be knocked off our horse of sin or blinded by what we think is right. What is your horse? One of my horses was that I thought I could fix the business with my money, gifts, and talents. I mistakenly believed I could have conquered the latter without fully depending on God.

As I previously stated, we seemed to have been at a standstill in our business, not moving forward. Finally, I realized God was included in my business plan, but He was not first in the plan. I would always say He is God and first in my life, however my actions were not in line with my confessions. God was getting the leftovers because I was so busy.

Finally I got it. If God is absent or not put first in my business plan, I will not receive the full manifestation of my purposefulness and destiny here on earth. One example of failing to achieve purpose is the inability to move our business to the next level. An example of God's blessing is seen in the fact that over the process of editing this book, we were awarded a grant to expand our program services to the community.

People may say, "It is easy for you to talk, because you have the skills and/or the education."

Well, I did not always have the skills or the education. I had a beginning, and we all have beginnings. While growing up, my self-esteem was low. I had great parents, but let's face the truth. Parents don't always say what is right. My dad told me I was an average student and he only expected "C's" from me. As a result that was all I gave him. I had some aspirations, but I was too afraid and doubted myself. Getting ready to graduate from high school, I was interested in working for the airlines. I waited for the requested information in the mail. The recruiter was in my neighborhood and asked to come by my house. I was so scared that I told him no. I asked him to just send me the information through the mail. Well, he never did, and that was one opportunity "out the door."

I listened to my mom and went to junior college. I said to myself, "I better be able to get a job once I finish." I had my first government job at nineteen. Time progressed and I obtained a Master's degree. I was so afraid on the job when I had to meet with the new management team. I felt so inadequate, therefore, my input was limited when I was asked a question. They seemed to have more years of experience, especially in juvenile delinquency.

Later, I overcame my lack of confidence through prayer and positive self-talk, such as, "I am just as good as the next person."

So if you are experiencing doubt or fear, one of my favorite scriptures is, "I can do all things through Christ who strengthens me." (Philippians 4:13) In believing this, I must continuously go before God daily in prayer, with humility and praise. Believe me, He will renew your strength like He has renewed mine. He will equip you with a vision and plan to obtain your purposefulness and destiny in this life on earth. Even though we have role models who inspire us, always remember our purpose and destiny come through Jesus the Christ who orchestrates our passion, dreams, talents, and interests that will be pleasing to God.

Another reason to pray is not just for ourselves; it is imperative that we pray for others. "Therefore I exhort first of all that supplications, prayers, intercessions, and giving of thanks be made for all men, for kings and all who are in authority, that we may lead a quiet and peaceable life in all godliness and reverence." (1Timothy 2:1) Paul is telling us what should be included in the prayer life of a church. Supplication is praying for personal needs, and prayers are always directed toward God with praise, reverence and worship. Intercession should be made in confidence. Giving thanks is an attitude of gratitude. Paul says the church must pray for all believers and unbelievers, including kings, presidents, and all country leaders because their judgments and decisions affect society as a whole.

Do we realize the detriment or harm caused by poverty, wickedness, catastrophes, plagues, diseases, wars, rumors of wars, and other societal ills? As we continue to pray for the personal needs, intercession, and thanksgiving for all people let us also remember to specifically include law enforcement, schools, universities, hospitals, and jails. Then we are to pray for children, parents, families, safety, communities, for love, peace, the elderly, the sick, drug addicts, against wickedness in high places, rulers of darkness, and much more, with thanks to God for all people. Fervent or passionate prayer accomplishes great results. The Bible says, "The effective, fervent prayer of a righteous man avails much." (James 5:16a) Remember that this is so because of the power of the blood of Jesus. Also these instructions should be the prayer life of every believer at home and in our individual prayer time, wherever that may be.

Therefore, Jesus is our sustainer of life and it is through His shed blood that we have obtained a better covenant from God. In the next chapter we will talk about His blood. Now, it was previously mentioned that God's covenant with Abraham included, "in your seed all the nations will be blessed." We spoke about a preparation phase. The better and new covenant was acquired little by little. It was given to us by God through the family line, of Abraham to David, fourteen generations; David to the Israelites' captivity in Babylon, because of disobedience, another fourteen generations; and from Babylon to Christ; fourteen generations. It took forty-two generations before the manifestation of the better covenant. Imagine starting with Abraham, the father of all nations, then Isaac, Jacob, and on and on until we reach the forty-second generation, as outlined in Matthew 1:1-17?

Jesus was the forty-second generation, and with Him the preparation phase ended, with the one-time, better sacrifice now ready, the atonement for our sins. "'This is the new covenant that I will make with them after those days,' says the Lord: 'I will put My laws into their hearts, and in their minds I will write them. Their sins and their lawless deeds I will remember no more.' Now where there is remission of these, there is no longer an offering for sin." (Hebrews 10:16-18) This means full and final forgiveness, including salvation, has been achieved for you and me. We can find no greater love than God who sacrificed His only begotten Son, a willing participant who provides us with the new and better covenant.

The Old and New Testament Blood Sacrifice

God is "the Alpha and the Omega, the Beginning and the End, says the Lord." (Revelations 1:8a) This shows God's eternal power over all creation, revealing that He is Almighty. He also said, "You shall have no other gods before Me." (Exodus 20:3) "For I, the Lord your God, am a jealous God." (Exodus 20:5b)

He knew we were going to sin before the fall or sin of Adam. He knew Adam was weak and would make the wrong decision. "If we say that we have no sin, we deceive ourselves, and the truth is not in us. If we confess our sins, He is faithful and just to forgive our sins and to cleanse us from all unrighteousness." (1 John 1:8-9)

In this chapter we will focus on the temporary sin offerings, known as the Day of Atonement in the Old Testament and the sacrifice of Jesus' blood in the New Testament.

God had given His commandments to Moses for the Israelites to obey. God knew the people would fail to keep His commands. Their disobedience was demonstrated in the wilderness and throughout their history. Therefore, sin offerings were instituted by God for the people to make atonement for the forgiveness of their sins. For example, if the whole congregation sinned unintentionally and it became known, the assembly had to offer a young bull for the sin and take the bull before the tabernacle. For all intents and purposes, there was a process for administering the sin offering. Normally, the elders laid their hands on the head of the bull before the Lord. Then the bull was killed. The anointed priest dipped his finger in the blood and sprinkled it seven times before the Lord, in front of the veil in the tabernacle. The number seven was used because it represents completeness. Finally, the bull was taken outside of the camp and burned. If the priest unintentionally sinned, he had to make atonement for himself first, in a similar fashion, before making atonement for the people. Animals used in the sin sacrifices included young pigeons, rams, goats, and lambs (Leviticus).

Aaron was the only one anointed as the high priest, since his sons Nadab and Abihu died. His other two sons, Eleazar and Ithamar, ministered as priests in the presence of Aaron. The tribe of Levi served as spiritual leaders and consisted of 22,000 males of their father's house (tribes) with the youngest barely a month old. Moses was commanded by God to bring the Levites closer, and they were responsible for serving Aaron and his sons, as well as serving in the tabernacle to meet the needs of the whole congregation before the tabernacle meeting. In addition, they were responsible for attending to the tabernacle furnishings such as the tent, its covering, screens for the doors, hangings of the court, pillars, the ark, table, lamp stand, altars, utensils of the sanctuary, and other duties (Numbers 3:14-38).

Among the Levite descendants of Aaron the priest, no man with a defect on his body could serve as a priest or serve the congregation in making atonement for sins or other offerings (Leviticus 21:21-23). Their bodies had to be perfect, without blemish, like the animal sacrifices. Thank God we are not living under the law or before Jesus died. Can you envision not being able to serve in the church as a deacon, pastor, minister, elder, or priest because of a bad leg, blindness, bad skin, being too short, having a broken hand, bad teeth, or any other kind of body defect?

Further, before anyone could have served in this office, they had to be consecrated by washing with water or sprinkling of water, washing their clothes, shaving their bodies, putting on priesthood garments, the ephod, and making burnt and sin offerings (Numbers 8:5-12). The priests and their sons were commanded, "Do not drink wine or intoxicating drink, you nor your sons with you, when you go into the tabernacle of meeting, lest you die. It shall be a statute forever throughout your generations that you may distinguish between holy and unholy, and between unclean and clean." (Leviticus 10:8-11)

It is important for today's church to be distinguished as holy. The world should see a difference between the church and the un-church, between the believer and the unbeliever. Christians are particularly watched by the person who is not living a life committed to God. How we present ourselves affects others; it can cause them to sin or not believe in Christ. We should always present our bodies as a living sacrifice, holy and acceptable unto God. Otherwise, we are labeled hypocrites. We must make up our minds to follow Christ wherever we may go. Every aspect of our lives should demonstrate an example of Christ.

It was the eighth day, after God had told Moses to call Aaron, his sons, the elders, and the congregation together, to make sin and burnt offerings of bulls and rams without blemish. The Israelites offered other unblemished animals including kids, calves, and lambs as peace, burnt, and grain offerings. Once they completed all the sacrifices, the anointing of the tabernacle and all of its contents, the glory of the Lord appeared by fire, and the people shouted and fell on their faces (Leviticus 9:24).

Notice the people could not present any kind of animal to God. Their animal sacrifices had to be specific, without spot, or wrinkle. They presented their best before God. I must seize this moment to iterate under the new covenant, Jesus is God's best, a sacrifice without a spot or wrinkle (sinless). Since Jesus has cleansed us from our sins, we must come before Him in prayer with repentance, our best in worship, praise, and thanksgiving. Hence, according to His word, we will enter into the place where He is and experience His fire and power while in His presence. We should seek to emulate the Israelites by repenting, shouting, falling on our faces, prostrating before God, and fully exalting Him as Lord of lords and King of kings.

Continuing to explore the significance of the blood, there were various types of blood offerings according to the type of sin and whether the sin was committed by a woman, man, or priest. The schedule for sin offerings included every morning, evening, each Sabbath, at the new moon, during festivals, and on the Day of Atonement (Theological Dictionary of the New Testament). Millions of animal sacrifices were made repeatedly.

The Passover and Feast of Unleavened (without yeast) Bread was the most important annual festivals among the Israelites. The Passover was instituted by God in memory of Israel's preservation from the last plague upon Egypt prior to their deliverance from bondage. I am sure you remember the story where Pharaoh would not let the people go. This was the final plague. Moses told the people to take a male lamb, without blemish, from their sheep or goats of the first year. At twilight (nightfall), they were instructed to kill the lamb, take some of its blood and put it on the two doorposts and lintel of the houses where they were to eat (Exodus 12:6-7). "For I will pass through the land of Egypt on that night, and will strike all the firstborn in the land of Egypt, both man and beast; and against all the gods of Egypt I will execute judgment: I am the Lord. Now the blood shall be a sign for you on the houses where you are. And when I see the blood, I will pass over you; and the plague shall not be on you to destroy you when I strike the land of Egypt. So this day shall be to you a memorial; and you shall keep it as a feast to the Lord throughout your generations." (Exodus 12:12-14b)

The blood sprinkled on the doorposts was the sign that the participants in the Passover were being sheltered from death through the death of the sacrificed lamb. We can compare this to the shed blood of Christ, the physical sign of a life given as a sacrifice so that humanity might be released from death and reconciled to God (The Layman Bible Encyclopedia).

Time continued to pass and the prophet Isaiah spoke about the judgment and idolatrous lifestyle of the Israelites. "To what purpose is the multitude of your sacrifices to Me? Says the Lord, I have had enough of burnt offerings of rams and the fat of fed cattle. I do not delight in the blood of bulls, or of lambs or goats. When you spread out your hands, I will hide My eyes from you; even though you make many prayers, I will not hear. Your hands are full of blood. Wash yourselves, make yourselves clean; put away the evil of your doings from before My eyes. Cease to do evil, learn to do good; seek justice, rebuke the oppressor, defend the fatherless, and plead for the widow." (Isaiah 1: 11, 15-17)

This is a message for the modern-day church to seek justice, rebuke the oppressor, defend the fatherless, and plead for the widow. Pure religion does not merely give material goods for the relief of the distressed; it also oversees their care (James 1:27). Jesus said, "I was hungry and you gave Me food, I was thirsty and you gave Me drink; I was a stranger and you took Me in; I was naked and you clothed Me; I was sick and you visited Me; I was in prison and you came to Me. As much as you did it to one of the least of these, you did it to Me." This is what God expects from the body of Christ and believers. We are living in a time when it is unsafe to let strangers or people in general into our houses. However, as a body in Christ and as believers we may provide some type of support, such as a referral to a shelter ministry or a homeless facility (Matthew 25:35-46).

Regarding the New Testament blood sacrifice, Isaiah prophesied, "For unto us a Child is born, unto us a Son is given, and the government will be upon His shoulder. His name will be called Wonderful, Counselor, Mighty God, Everlasting Father, and Prince of Peace. There will be no end, upon the throne of David and over His kingdom, to order it and establish it with judgment and justice, from that time forward, even forever." (Isaiah 9:6-7a) The prophet explained that Jesus is the one who will establish the new covenant in the line of David. Therefore, He came in the form of a baby to fulfill that which was promised. The time had arrived for the ultimate sacrifice. Visualize the Power of the Blood of Jesus.

For a point of reference we will begin with Calvary where the crown of thorns was made out of a thorny plant that was intentionally thrust into Jesus' head. Imagine the blood streaming down from His head to His face and neck? The Bible says the soldiers mocked Jesus, spit on Him, and hit Him on the head. He was crucified (Matthew 27:29-34). Crucifixion was considered the most horrible form of death. The cross that Jesus was nailed and tied to was probably three or four feet from the ground. Jesus' hands and feet were nailed and bound to the cross. He was offered a medicated drink that was probably mixed with wine and myrrh to confuse His senses and deaden the pounding nails through His body. Jesus refused the drink so that His senses would be clear. At another point He was offered a sponge filled with sour wine on a reed. The Bible says that He probably accepted it for strength (Matthew 27:48). Otherwise, He bore the pain. His blood flowed down, staining His body, the cross, and the ground. He was pierced in His side. Blood stains covered His back from the thirty-nine stripes that He took for us. Jesus' shed blood was given for our sins and so much more (Theological Dictionary of the New Testament).

Think about Jesus' blood in comparison to the tabernacle where the high priest made offerings for the sins of the people. The tabernacle is also mentioned in Chapter 5. The cross where Jesus was nailed, where He was given for a sacrifice or ransom by God, is like the altar where animal sacrifices were made. The saturated and stained blood of Jesus on His body, the cross and ground represents the sprinkling of animal blood on the altar. Jesus was the perfect Lamb, a sacrifice of God without blemish, spot, wrinkle or sin. At Calvary, the designated location for His death where the cross was placed represents the tabernacle, the Holy Place, the Holies of Holy where the high priest had to enter into once a year, the Day of Atonement for the sin offerings. However, Jesus' blood is the ultimate, one-time sacrifice, the one and only divine life for many lives to save sinners like you and me until the end of time.

We are still talking about the power of the blood, the majestic or royal creation of the only wise, true and invisible Lord, our God. Remember, blood is the sustainer of life. Let not Jesus' shed blood be in vain or of no importance to us. When we accept Jesus the Christ as our Lord and Savior, the Bible declares that our hearts are cleansed from all of our sins by His shed blood. Then we have the right to take the authority and declare the Power of the Blood at work in our lives. The power is most importantly needed if we desire to endure life circumstances in peace, love, joy, and purposefulness.

Significance of the Broken Veil

The significance of the broken veil was vital for the people to communicate with God again, have their sins forgiven, and become benefactors of God's new covenant. The priests lead the people astray, accepting blemished animal sacrifices to present to God for the atonements of their sins. The people failed to obey God's commandments that were given to them by Moses and worshipped false gods. They oppressed the poor and the fatherless. They simply lived unjustly. Therefore, God no longer delighted in the Israelites (Isaiah 1:1-17).

When we think about the Israelites or the priests and their behavior, we need to realize that God did not require any more of them than He requires of Himself. He is not the type of God who says 'do what I say, not what I do.' God is righteous and holy. God served as an example to the Israelites through the many deadly deeds done to the Egyptians in their presence. The Egyptians blessed them with silver, gold, and other valuables as they departed Egypt. God parted the sea twice and fed them in the wilderness. In spite of God's blessings, the Israelites continued to sin and took God for granted.

What about us? I believe we are so spoiled when it comes to taking the things of God more seriously. We continue in the same old sin, such as unrighteous living, while God continues to exhibit His compassion and love. Hypothetically, if we had a time machine that would take us back to the days of the Old Testament, I believe life for us would be very miserable and unbearable. I cannot imagine living in a time where people fell dead because of disobedience, making bricks in Egypt, or living in the wilderness. What about you?

God put His laws in place to prevent the Israelites from sinning and a reminder to live holy. In addition, God required the presentation of animal sacrifices without a blemish. He expected the priests who performed the sin offering ceremonies to present themselves holy and pure before Him. When the priests sinned, they had to make atonement for themselves first. God, being a holy God, All-Knowingly, the Holiest of Holy who hates sin, knew the animal sacrifices were not good enough, unacceptable, and could not save mankind from sin. Therefore, He promised His son, Jesus as a living sacrifice for the people's sins and more. A better way was prophesied for God's people. The Angel of the Lord told Abraham, "In your seed all the nations of the earth shall be blessed, because you have obeyed My voice." (Genesis 22: 18) God also made a covenant with Isaac and Jacob, Abraham's descendants to King David to Jesus, the King who will rule forever (Genesis 22: 17-18; 24:25-26 & Isaiah 9:6-7a).

Jesus came on the scene to fulfill His purpose as the perfect Lamb without a blemish or sin for the atonement of mankind's sins and more. The Bible says, "And Jesus cried out with a loud voice, and breathed His last." He died, a willing participant and the one-time sacrifice by crucifixion, a sin offering for all mankind. Jesus died for the believers as well as for the unbelievers.

Today, we have the best opportunity to live a holy life that is acceptable to God. This is because of the new covenant through Jesus' shed blood and the tearing of the veil in the temple. When Jesus died, the temple veil was torn in two from top to bottom (Mark 15:37a-38). Behind the veil was the Holy of Holies, also known as the Most Holy Place.

The significance of the Holy of Holies was where the presence of God dwelled. It was God's special dwelling place in the midst of His people. The Holy of Holies was a sacred room, a place no ordinary person could enter except for the anointed priest. A thick curtain separated the Holy of Holies from the Holy Place. This curtain, as the "veil," was made of fine linen and gold, blue, purple and scarlet yarn. There were figures of cherubim angels embroidered onto it. The cherubim spirits served God and were in His presence demonstrating His almighty power. The Holy of Holies represented Heaven. The throne of God was guarded and the cherubim angels were on the innermost layer of the tent covering (Theological Dictionary of the New Testament).

The veil was a barrier between man and God, revealing God's holiness and indicating that He could not be tampered with. God's eyes are too pure to look on evil, and He can tolerate no sin (Habakkuk 1:13). The veil was an assurance that

POWER OF THE BLOOD AT WORK "BROKEN VEIL"   77

man could not carelessly and irresponsibly enter into God's awesome presence. Remember, Moses set up parameters around Mount Sinai when God showed His presence among the children of Israel. The parameters were to keep the people from touching its base and climbing the mountain. If the people had attempted to touch the base or climb the mountain, they would have been put to death. Further, the people could not go before God looking any kind of way. They had to consecrate themselves by going through a ceremony and washing their clothes before going near Mount Sinai (Exodus 19:10-13).

Back to the Holy of Holies, the high priest was the only one permitted to pass through the veil. All others would die. This prescribed event was the "Day of Atonement." The anointed high priest entered past the veil, offering the atonement for the people's sins. This occurred only once a year (Hebrews 9:7). The high priest had to prepare himself before entering into the Holy of Holies. He had to bathe, put on special clothing, and bring burning incense into the Holy of Holies to let the smoke cover his eyes from a direct view of God.

The presence of God remained shielded from man behind a thick curtain during the history of Israel. When Jesus died, the curtain in the Jerusalem temple was torn in half or in two, from the top to the bottom. Only God could have carried out such an incredible feat because the veil was too high for human hands to have reached it, and too thick for human hands to tear. The Jerusalem temple was a replica of the wilderness tabernacle. The veil was about 60 feet in height, 30 feet in width and 4 inches thick. As the veil was torn, the Holy of Holies was exposed. The Holy of Holies is a representation of heaven itself. It is God's dwelling place (Theological Dictionary of the New Testament).

Even though there are three Heavens, emphasis will be placed on the third Heaven (2 Corinthians 2:2), which is the dwelling place of the Father, Son, and Holy Spirit. Heaven is called glory, since Christ is crowned with glory and honor (Hebrew 2:7, 10); and a place of beauty (Revelations 21:10-22:7), of life (1 Timothy 4:8-10), service (Revelation 22:3), and worship (Revelation 19:1-5). Through the broken veil, which is like heaven, we now have access to God for ourselves, as often as we want to approach Him. This access is made available by the shed blood of Jesus (Hebrews 2:9), who has returned to Heaven, our High Priest with our Father making our prayers known and interceding on our behalf to God (Hebrews 4:14-16).

Benefits of the Blood of Jesus

6

God's presence is now accessible to all. It is good news to us as believers, because we know that the blood of Jesus was and still is an atonement or offering for our sins, making us right before God. The torn veil illustrated Jesus' broken body, opening the way for us to go before God ourselves. Jesus cried out "it is finished" on the cross. He was indeed proclaiming that God's redemptive plan to deliver man from sin was now complete. The age of animal offerings was over. Jesus, the ultimate offering, had been sacrificed (Hebrews 6:19-20).

We now have Jesus the Christ as our High Priest over the house of God (Hebrews 10:21a). "'This is the covenant that I will make with them after those days, says the Lord. I will put My laws into their hearts, and in their minds I will write them,' then He adds, 'Their sins and their lawless deeds I will remember no more.'" (Hebrews 10:16-17) "Now where there is remission of these, there is no longer an offering for sin." (Hebrews 10:18)

In other words, the new covenant is the grace given to mankind by God. It is a gift, something we did not earn or work for. God's grace provides not only salvation, but safety and preservation for the ones saved, despite our imperfections. Grace perfects forever the saved, in the sight of God, because of our position in Christ. Therefore, God said, He remembers our sins or lawless deeds no more. This grace is for all mankind, beginning with Adam and forevermore (Theological Dictionary of the New Testament).

Are we to continue in sin because of God's grace? Paul says "certainly not!" (Romans 6:15) God is still calling us to a higher standard of living, even though we are not living under the law of the old covenant. God loves us so much that He has given us grace. He does not remember our sin, but to receive God's grace we must be saved. It is not automatic. However, it is available for everyone. I believe He has made it easy for us to obtain salvation. We can compare God's grace to having brand new shoes or a new suit given to us that we should accept and put on.

Therefore, once we repent and accept Christ as our Lord and Savior, the benefit of His blood is salvation. According to the New Testament, salvation comes from the love of God and is based on the atonement or the covering of our sins by the blood of Jesus. Through salvation we have forgiveness, regeneration, justification, and sanctification. This means:

- Forgiveness of our sins through Jesus, the ultimate blood sacrifice. Once we repent, God remembers our sins no more. This is because of His grace.

- Regeneration is to be born again or born of God; to accept Christ as our Lord and Savior. A character change, because the Holy Spirit is activated and lives within our hearts.

- Justification is a change in our relation to God. This change is from spiritual death to spiritual life.

- Sanctification is the believer's separation from the secular (world) and sin, and is set apart for a sacred purpose to be used by God. Our true purpose on earth is to be used by God. The scriptures, power, and significance of Jesus' blood are indicated below:

- "In Him we have salvation through His blood, the forgiveness of sins, according to the riches of His grace which He made to abound toward us in all wisdom and prudence, having made known to us the mystery of His will, according to His good pleasure which He purposed in Himself… In Him also we have obtained an inheritance, being predestined according to the purpose of Him who works all things according to the counsel of His will." (Ephesians 1:7-9, 11)

Once we have salvation, God lives inside of us. If we submit ourselves to do His will, He will give us an understanding of His word, clarify matters for us, and show us how to obtain our destiny that is pleasing to Him. He does not expect for us to be perfect, but He will help us in those areas that we know are not pleasing to Him. Are we an extremist in drinking or cursing? Sometimes we may feel that to emulate Jesus' life is boring. There is fun in Jesus. However, we must first be in Jesus to experience the fun. A person must examine them self and ask, Is God pleased with the way I live my life? If not, He is not going to wave a magic wand over anyone's head. Your decision is a personal choice to follow God or continue in the ways that are displeasing to Him. Remember, He hates sin, and there are promises in living a life that is pleasing to Him. As for me, I need the victory in all areas of my life and success for my son, grandson, and generations to come.

- "Now may the God of peace who brought up our Lord Jesus from the dead, that great Shepherd of the sheep, through the blood of the everlasting covenant, make you complete in every good work to do His will, working in you what is well pleasing in His sight, through Jesus Christ, to whom be glory forever and ever." (Hebrews 13:20) Amen.

We are still talking about God's everlasting covenant with mankind through the ultimate sacrifice of Jesus' blood and His resurrection. We are known as the sheep in need of a Shepherd.

God does not expect for us to have it all together all of the time. Remember, Satan goes back and forth on earth to see who he can conquer (1 Peter 5:8). This is the reason that God gave His son, Jesus, as a living sacrifice. Therefore, a sheep is described as timid, fearful, vulnerable, jealous, and dumb. The Shepherd is needed because of its most effective and calming influence. God is compassionate and is waiting for us to accept Christ as our Great Shepherd. He wants to restore us to our rightful place before Adam sinned in the Garden of Eden (Genesis 1:26-31).

Once again, it is about choices. Maybe you are influenced by peer pressure, since many adults are part of groups, associations, or cliques that are not in God's will, or they are lukewarm Christians (Revelation 3:16). Sometimes we think children and youth are the only ones who give in to peer pressure, but adults certainly do, too. What happens when you need prayer? Do you feel there is power in your prayers? Would you ask someone to pray for you who seems to be living to please God or someone who loves God, but is not living to please Him? Remember, God want to do His perfect work in you and me.

- "Jesus took bread, blessed and broke it, and gave it to the disciples and said, take, eat; this is My body.' Then He took the cup, and gave thanks, and gave it to them, saying, 'Drink from it, all of you. For this is My blood of the new covenant, which is shed for many for the remission of sins." (Mathew 26:26b-28) We can also find these same words in Mark 14:22-24.

What love Christ has for all of us! The bread symbolizes Jesus' broken body for us, and He is also known as the "Bread of Life." The wine represents His blood sacrifice. This is the new covenant He has made for us, the forgiveness of our sins, and to remember them no more. Further, God said He will put His laws into our hearts and minds and will write them down. A question was asked earlier: Do you want the benefits of Jesus' blood to be of value to your life and your children's lives? With obedience there is a promise. You make the choice and set the standard. God said He will bless your house and your children from generation to generation. Do you want your family to be blessed until the end of time?

In other words, Jesus paid the price. The duties of the high priest in the Old Testament to offer animal blood sacrifices, to pass through the veil into the presence of God in the Holy of Holies, and to pray for the forgiveness of their sins and the people's sins ARE OVER.

There is no comparison to the benefits of the ultimate sacrifice, the power of Jesus' blood and His death. It was strong enough to tear the veil in two from top to bottom. Jesus is our Veil, Shepherd, Mediator, and High Priest. We now have access to God when we pray in the name of Jesus. We must believe that Jesus rose from the dead and is in the presence of God, the Holy of Holies. He makes our prayers known and intercedes daily on our behalf before God, our Heavenly Father.

How to Apply the 7
Power of the Blood of Jesus

Now the word of God has been spoken through scriptures, life experiences, and examples. It is my hope that you have a better understanding of the power of the blood of Jesus and its benefits. What good is the power of Jesus' blood and its benefits if we fail to take advantage of what God is offering us? The power of Jesus' blood is effective in applying over our strongholds. Strongholds are life situations that we deal with daily that seem to heavily weigh us down and "keep us on our knees." My strongholds or problems included being disobedient and too busy to hear God. The results or consequences were not having money to put gas in my car. I stopped answering the telephone because it made me frustrated to explain over and over again why my bills were not being paid. My mortgage was behind and bank accounts were closed for being overdrawn.

In prayer I called my strongholds or situations out by name. I cried out to the Lord in a position of repentance, humbleness, and submission. I continue to pray the power of Jesus' blood over my situation. Also, I decree and declare the solution in God's specific word to overcome life situations. The Bible tells us, "Yet in all these things we are more than conquerors, through Him who loved us." (Romans 8:37) Further, "If God is for us, who can be against us?" (Romans 8:31a) We must say what God's word say!

Some of your situations may be worse than mine. People may say, "Arnetha, you chose your situation, and you really have not hit rock bottom." Others may say, "Arnetha, you have an education and options." Whatever you may think, God allowed me to get in this place to humble me, to put Him first in my life and to realize the provisions already made for me through the power of Jesus' blood. Thank God! I did not have to hit rock bottom, because at some point God gave me another chance, and I choose to listen to Him. Remember, the work was completed when Jesus died on the cross, and because of God's grace, He remembers our sins no more. Even though we have God's grace, we must do something by continuing in prayer, listening, and applying His word daily in our lives.

We must pray without ceasing (1 Thessalonians 5:17). There are times when we may not feel like praying. My Pastor Cecil Lamb would always tell us at the Spirit of Christ Center & Ministries that, "It is not about how we feel, because feelings come and go." Here is one of my prayers, and I hope you find it helpful as you continue to grow in Christ:

Good Morning Lord, Blessed be Your name in all the earth and all the heavens. There is none like you. From the rising of the sun till it sets, there is none like You. O Lord, You are Alpha and Omega, the Beginning and the End. You are such a good God, an almighty God, and You are worthy to be praised. I just worship You, O Lord, in the beauty of Your holiness. I bow down before You. I just want to enter into Your presence, the Holy of Holies, that is where You are. I want to feel your power and glory. You showed up in the Israelites' camp even though they were a group of rebellious people. Daniel's prayers got through. O Lord, please hear me. What you have done for others, I believe You will do for me. I thank You. Then Father I thank You for Your grace and mercy. There is nothing I can do to earn Your grace; it is Your perfect gift to me, to the world, and I thank You. I thank You for the shed blood of Jesus. I thank You for the power that is in the blood of Jesus. I confess my sins before You. I repent for my wrongdoings, for not trusting You, for not leaning and depending on You and for not completing the assignments You have given me. I repent for my negative thoughts and negative speech. You said that if I repent, you will forgive my sins and remember them no more. So Lord, I thank You for washing me whiter than snow. I thank You for another chance to get right with You. I cannot do it without You. Please guide my thoughts and renew my mind in You.

Not just forgive me, O Lord, but forgive my son _____, my daughter _____, my grandson/granddaughter _____, my brothers/sisters

_____, other family members _____, my friends _____, my neighbors _____, the community, the body of Christ, those in authority in government, the United States, and the world. Forgive them for all of their sins. I declare that they come before You with repentance in their hearts for their wrongdoing, and You will forgive them. I thank You for the forgiveness of their sins.

I thank You that the price has already been paid and the victory has already been won through Christ Jesus' blood. Therefore, I plead the power of Jesus' blood over my life, situations, my family, friends, pastor, church, schools, business, government, Your people, and everything that concerns You. I plead the power of Jesus' blood over our hurts, pain, sickness, disappointments, disobedient children, broken relationships, lack of money or a job, our negative imagination, rulers of darkness, and wickedness in high places that try to weigh us down. The devil is a lie and the truth is not in him.

This is warfare and I/we are ready for the battle. I/we are equipped daily with our believer's protection. I/we wear the belt of truth where I/we stand for God, not for you, Satan. God protects my/our heart(s). I/we have on the breastplate of righteousness and maintain the righteousness of God, and in the name of Jesus the enemy shall flee. My/our feet are covered with the gospel of truth, and I/we have the shield of faith to put out every attack that comes against me/us. I/we have on the helmet of salvation, the forgiveness of my/our sins.

You can't hold me/us down, Satan, or make me/us feel guilty, because I/we are still a child of God and entitled to His benefits. I decree and declare God's word, and His word is powerful and effective to overcome every situation. The earth and everything in it belongs to You, God. So, my Lord and my King, I/we are standing on Your word for the release of Your blessings, release in healings, mended relationships, restoration, salvation for the lost, money, jobs, and the Fruit of Your Spirit. The devil in hell shall not prevail! After all I/we have done to stand, I/we shall continue to stand! I/we pray for the lost souls, Your people, that they be saved and come to an understanding that You are a God who loves them and cares. It is Your desire that all be saved and none be lost.

So, I/we thank You for the victory in this area. I/we thank You for hearing and answering my/our prayer. You said the prayers of the righteous avails much. I/we thank You, the Lord Most High and My King, for all that You are doing and for all that is to come. All my/our help comes from You. You are the Author and Finisher of my/our faith, from the rising of the sun to the going down of the same. You are worthy to be praised. You are worthy to be honored and glorified in all the earth. Oh, I/we just praise Your name and thank You for all of Your benefits. In Jesus' name I/we pray. Amen!

Feel free to use this prayer. In fact, this whole book can be a book of prayers by itself. I did not add any scriptures to the prayer since many of these scriptures are already quoted in this book. May this prayer be a blessing upon your life!

The scripture also says, "He will fulfill the desire of those who fear Him; He also will hear their cry and save them." (Psalm 145:19) Prayer includes praying in the Spirit (tongues). This is praying to

God in an unknown language, because many times we do not know what we should pray for. Therefore Jesus makes intercessions for us to God. He knows what we need to pray for. Sometimes God reveals to us the interpretation of our prayer in the Spirit. The scripture tells us to pray always with all prayer and supplication in the Spirit (Ephesians 6:18a).

Let us talk about the word "fear" of God. Since we are believers or unbelievers in Christ, sometimes we have difficulty understanding the meaning. To "fear" God is to dread His displeasure, desire His favor, reverence His holiness, submit cheerfully to His will, feel grateful for His benefits, sincerely worship Him, and conscientiously obey His commandments. The fear and love for God must operate together in our lives for a healthy relationship and so that we may rightly serve Him (Theological Dictionary of the New Testament). It was mentioned earlier that the greatest commandment is, "You shall love the Lord your God with all your heart, with all your soul, and with all your mind." (Matthew 22:37)

This book is alive, real, and powerful to me because it is helping me to press through, depend on God, and trust Him to meet all of my needs through the benefits of Jesus' blood. I can remember after praying on the very same day of September 29, I received a telephone call that a check was available to pay staff and some of my bills; that lifted my burden. Oh, we are not out of the wilderness yet, but we are on our way.

Earlier I said that little by little, I will receive more of God's blessings, just like the Israelites who entered into the Promised Land. I am still in the preparation phase of my life; however, I have grown spiritually. Maybe you have too. Our spiritual growth is a continuous cycle. We must constantly stay in prayer, talk to God, and seek Him to do His will in our lives.

God has made His benefits available to us through salvation. We have the forgiveness of our sins and are born again when we accept Jesus as our Lord and Savior. We should have a change in our moral and spiritual nature by the Holy Spirit. We must have a spiritual life that is godly, different from the ways of people in the world. See 1 John 2:15-17 to learn how we should live to please God. It is important to join a good teaching church to help develop one's spiritual growth.

My toolkit to please God started over ten years ago. I feel that the toolkit for each of us is tailor-made according to our life experiences, the motivation for change, and a commitment to change or improve our spiritual walk with God.

- I identified a need to change because I wanted favor from God and realized He needed something from me in return: A more righteous and holy life.

- I am a confessed believer in Jesus the Christ.

- I read the Bible for myself to better understand what God is saying.

- I take the pastor's message seriously and make an effort to live by God's word.

- I limited my partying in clubs, until I no longer enjoy partying in the clubs.

- I stopped drinking, except for wine or champagne on special occasions one to three times per year.

- I formally pray an average of twice daily.

- I teach in the youth church, and through studying my faith has enhanced.

- Over a period of time, I grew more godly on the inside and it manifested on the outside. This means that because the Holy Spirit lives inside me, it's easier for me to live to please God. The hindrances came from past relationships. However, because of the Holy Spirit I have the ability to remain committed and steadfast. As a result I witness break-throughs and God's favor. Life continues to bring new challenges, but my faith has increased through prayer.

- I plead the blood and now the power of Jesus' blood over my life, situation, family, pastors, churches, communities, countries and much more.

- I declare what God says about my life, quoting scriptures for success.

- Most times I do not engage in negative talk regarding the business or family.

- I am learning to trust God more.

- I praise, worship, and thank God more.

- I have learned how to demonstrate the Fruit of the Spirit more.

I feel that, based on my toolkit or self-assessment, the most common factors for everyone are a willing heart and a commitment to a more righteous and holy lifestyle. A real and genuine change must start from the heart with the desire to please God. One must be a confess believer in Jesus the Christ. We must read the Bible and pray more. We must decree and declare God's specific word, including the blood and the power of Jesus' blood over our life, circumstances, mind, body, and others for deliverance, restoration, breakthrough, forgiveness, salvation, healing, and success according to God's will. We should join a good teaching church, praise, worship, and give reverence to God daily. Finally, we must demonstrate the Fruit of the Spirit operating in our lives which includes love, joy, kindness, patience, and longsuffering. I am sure God is already using you to bless others in ways that are beyond your imagination. Nothing that we do for God is too great or too small. He desires to use all of us more and more because of the finished work of Jesus. The greatest provision available for you and I are through Jesus' shed blood, along with the resulting benefits. God loves us so much that we can enter into His presence, the Holy of Holies, by praying in Jesus' name. Jesus the Christ is where God is, sitting on the right hand side of our Father. He serves as our Broken Veil, Mediator, Great Shepherd, and High Priest going before God daily on our behalf (Hebrews 10:21a).

We must remember, "But seek first the kingdom of God and His righteousness, and all these things shall be added to you." (Matthew 6:33) Therefore, I now trust God more for my business, finances, husband, children, and family. This is the "Power of the Blood at Work" in my life through the "Broken Veil."

Glossary

Abase is to be without or suffer need.

Abound is to have plenty of or flourish.

Atonement is the covering over of sin, a covenant, the reconciliation between God and man accomplished by the Lord Jesus Christ. It is that special result of Christ's sacrificial sufferings and death.

Believers are Christians who demonstrate their faith in the person and the work of Jesus.

Christ means the Anointed one of God as the Prophet, High Priest, and King.

Covenants are various promises or agreements God made to His servants, or to man, and their descendants.

Fruit of the Spirit refers to love, joy, peace, longsuffering, kindness, goodness, faithfulness, gentleness, and self-control, attributes we can develop through Christ Jesus.

God refers to the two essential and personal names of God are Elohim and Jehovah. However, more correctly the name is Yahweh, which means fullness of divine power, He who is declaring the divine self-existence.

Prayer is intercession, supplication for another, plea, request, petition, and communicating with God from the heart.

Praying in the Spirit (tongues) is praying to God in an unknown language, an utterance given by the Holy Spirit.

Propitiation is an offering for the sins of man. This is what Jesus became for man, our sin offering.

Salvation is the forgiveness of sin, regeneration, justification, sanctification, the love of God, and having power and dominion over sin.

Satan is the chief fallen spirit, the devil, the evil one, the ruler of this world, the prince of the power of the air, darkness, the adversary.

Workbook

This workbook was developed as a study guide for several reasons:

- To help us understand the Power of the Blood at Work and the results of the Broken Veil.

- To access and apply this book in our lives toward building a closer relationship with God.

- To receive God's full benefits on earth and blessings for our families from generation to generation.

- To build God's kingdom and receive eternal life.

Exercise 1
Self-Assessment

Directions:
Please rate your opinion on a scale from (a) strongly disagree to (e) strongly agree by circling one answer per question. This self-assess how you feel about your spiritual development and how this book has been of benefit to you.

There are no wrong or right answers. One's spiritual development is personal and begins right where you are. Thank you for taking the time to complete your assessment. May God continue to bless you as you continue to grow spiritually, and may you have fun doing so.

1. Before reading this book, I was satisfied with my spiritual development.
    a. strongly disagree
    b. disagree
    c. neutral
    d. agree
    e. strongly agree

2. Since reading this book, I am inspired to increase my spiritual development.
   a. strongly disagree
   b. disagree
   c. neutral
   d. agree
   e. strongly agree

3. There are some specific things about my life that I need to change.
   a. strongly disagree
   b. disagree
   c. neutral
   d. agree
   e. strongly agree

4. I am more serious about the power of Jesus' blood.
   a. strongly disagree
   b. disagree
   c. neutral
   d. agree
   e. strongly agree

5. I know my purpose in life is to please God.
   a. strongly disagree
   b. disagree
   c. neutral
   d. agree
   e. strongly agree

6. My plan or vision is written down.
   a. strongly disagree
   b. disagree
   c. neutral
   d. agree
   e. strongly agree

7. I trust God to meet all of my needs.
   a. strongly disagree
   b. disagree
   c. neutral
   d. agree
   e. strongly agree

8. I try to please God in everything that I do.
   a. strongly disagree
   b. disagree
   c. neutral
   d. agree
   e. strongly agree

9. I believe God wants to use me more.
    a. strongly disagree
    b. disagree
    c. neutral
    d. agree
    e. strongly agree

10. I am ready to be used more by Jesus.
    a. strongly disagree
    b. disagree
    c. neutral
    d. agree
    e. strongly agree

Exercise 2

Directions:

Rank in the order of 1, 2, 3, etc. from the most important (#1) to the least (#6), areas that you need to improve in, and state why. You can always add more areas and ranks:

Rank	Areas	Why
	Pray More	
	Read Bible	
	Study More	
	Habits	
	Friends	
	Go To Church	

Exercise 3

Indicate the reason(s) that many of the Israelites did not receive the Promised Land:

_____
_____
_____
_____
_____
_____
_____
_____

How do you feel about the Israelites and their behavior during the time they were in the wilderness?

_____
_____
_____
_____
_____
_____
_____
_____

Exercise 4

Name five things you learned about the blood:

_____
_____
_____
_____
_____

In your own words, write your prayer using the power of the blood of Jesus:

_____
_____
_____
_____
_____
_____
_____
_____
_____
_____
_____
_____

Exercise 5

Indicate one important issue or situation that you believe God for:

_____
_____
_____

Indicate your stronghold(s) that could interfere or keep you from receiving what you ask God for:

_____
_____
_____
_____

List at least three scriptures and where they can be found in the Bible to support what you believe God for. Confess your scriptures daily for your breakthrough:

_____
_____
_____
_____
_____
_____

Exercise 6

Imagine your losses such as money, job, friends, or relationships and explain how you would or have handled your losses:

_____
_____
_____
_____
_____
_____
_____
_____

In the book of Job, we see that Satan went before God and God told Satan what kind of person Job was. He said Job was upright, blameless, and feared God. If God had to tell Satan about you, what would He say?

_____
_____
_____
_____
_____
_____

Exercise 7

Pre-Question:

Do you know your purpose or passion? (check only one)

☐ yes ☐ no ☐ unsure

Indicate what you are good at:

_____
_____
_____
_____
_____
_____
_____
_____
_____
_____

Indicate your purpose (passion). If you do not know, you can answer this question later:

_____
_____

Indicate how your purpose/passion pleases God:

Exercise 8

We talked about a vision or plan and making it plain by writing it down. My vision or plan is:

_____

_____

_____

_____

_____

I plan to accomplish my plan or vision by the following date:

_____

These are the steps I will take to complete my plan or vision:

1. _____
by _____

2. _____
by _____

3. _____
by _____

4. _____
by _____

5. _____
by _____

Use words (for example, satisfied, bored, happy, etc.) to describe how content you are in the areas below. Once you have completed the exercise, think about or compare your responses to Paul's point of view. The Bible says that he learned how to cope regardless of his situation.

Career choice

_____

Job

_____

Home

_____

Relationships

_____

Spiritual development

_____

Overall attitude

_____

Other (state) _____
& Description

_____

Which do you prefer to live under, the law or the new covenant? Why?

_____
_____
_____
_____
_____
_____
_____
_____
_____
_____
_____
_____
_____

Exercise 9

Name five things you learned about the broken veil:

1. _____
2. _____
3. _____
4. _____
5. _____

A Test of Your Remembrance

What was Paul's original name? _____
Paul said be strong in the _____ and the
_____ of His might._____
the evil one wants to control us. Name three of the
armor of God: _____,
_____, and
_____. Jesus said the greatest
commandment is: _____
_____
_____

Write the vision down and make it_____
_____ on tablets. Moses knew
God as _____. What did Asaph
say about God?_____
_____

Who was Asaph? _____
_____. God is faithful and always makes a
way of _____ .
Arnetha knew God was speaking to her through
_____.
Little by little is the_____

phase. God wants all to be _____ and none lost. Indicate two reasons why this book was written: _____

_____

_____

The blood sustains life in the _____ and _____.

Name two things you learned about the Tabernacle:

_____

_____

What happened to the veil when Jesus took His last breath and died?

_____

_____

_____

_____

_____

Are you trusting God more and, if so, in what ways?

_____

_____

_____

_____

What is Salvation?

Describe the benefits of the power of Jesus' blood:

Describe at least three ways this book may have changed your life:

Commitment Contract
Building My Relationship With God

Directions:

Please read and complete. Review weekly to assess whether or not you are on target. Revise as needed.

I _____,
commit to the following:

List up to 3 goals that will help build your relationship with God. For instance, I will pray more.

1. _____

_____

2. _____

_____

3. _____

_____

The steps or what I will do to build my relationship with God, including target dates for completing each step, are:

1. _____
_____

2. _____
_____

3. _____
_____

_____ _____
Signature   Date

Contract Review Sheet

Date	Comments

About the Author

Arnetha is just an ordinary person blessed by God to do extraordinary things. She grew up in the church and her testimony is similar to that of many for whom "the church was not in her." Through life experiences and God's grace, her spiritual development grew.

Arnetha , a licensed, ordained minister, faithfully sits under the teachings of her Pastor Cecil Lamb. Further, Reverend Gerry Latson taught Arnetha that she must present herself approved by God as a worker not ashamed, but rightly dividing the word of truth, as confirmed in 2 Timothy 2:15. She gives all thanks to God for the memories of her mother's love, nurturing, and serving as a role-model in her life. These are the most important attributes that have influenced Arnetha's spiritual foundation. Even though she drifted away from her earlier teachings of Christ, she was never to the point of no return, because of the mother given to her by God, as well as His grace and mercy.

During Arnetha's prayer and mediation with God, it seems although she was traveling upward and experienced a sound like wind in her right ear.

Please note this ear was stopped-up and had been for months. As Arnetha was traveling, she said "Okay God, I don't know where You are taking me, but I'm just going to ride with you." Arnetha rode it out with God and He said to her, "I will open up your ear, so that you will be able to hear and understand My word. Instantly Arnetha's right ear popped and has not been clogged since that time. Thus, Arnetha is trusting God for her writings and He has given her more books to write about Him, His word, and the application of His word in our lives.

She serves with a number of ministries in capacities that include youth leader, intercessor, and head of the Father's Ministry.

Arnetha graduated from Miami Northwestern Senior High School, ranked 166 out of a class of 534 students. She took courses at Miami Dade Community College and later earned a Master's Degree in Social Work from Barry University. She is a Family Mediator, practitioner of National Restorative Justice and Kingian Non-violence, Peer Mediation Trainer; and conference speaker.

She is the Founder and Chief Executive Officer of Solid Rock Enterprise, Inc., a non-profit organization utilizing the Restorative Justice Model for schools and communities to effectively deter children and youth referrals to the juvenile justice system, hold the students accountable for their behaviors, build and mend broken relationships, enhance safety, and competency development. Her vision is a community of hope, healing, and harmony.

Arnetha, born and raised in Miami Dade County, is the mother of Darius and the grandmother of Darius II.

To contact author:

U4lifemedia at:
305 705-2026 & 888 712-1985

Facebook or Twitter:
U4lifemedia@yahoo.com

www.solidrockent.org

www.ingramcontent.com/pod-product-compliance
Lightning Source LLC
Chambersburg PA
CBHW051449290426

44109CB00016B/1685